# The National Poetry Series

*The National Poetry Series* was established in 1978 to ensure the
publication of five poetry books annually through five participating
publishers. Publication is funded by the Lannan Foundation;
Stephen Graham; Joyce & Seward Johnson Foundation; Glenn and
Renee Schaeffer, Juliet Lea Hillman Simonds Foundation; and
Charles B. Wright III.

**DATE DUE**

2008 COMPETITION

**Anna Journey of Houst**
Chosen by Thomas Lux,

**Douglas Kearney of Van**
Chosen by Catherine W

**Adrian Matejka of Edw**
Chosen by Kevin Young

**Kristin Naca of Minnea**
Chosen by Yusef Komu
**Prize,** to be published b

**Sarah O'Brien of Brook**
Chosen by David Shapi

*If Birds Gather Your Hair for Nesting*

# If Birds Gather Your Hair for Nesting

POEMS BY Anna Journey

The University of Georgia Press ⁓ *Athens & London*

Published by the University of Georgia Press
Athens, Georgia 30602
www.ugapress.org
© 2009 by Anna Journey
All rights reserved
Designed by Erin Kirk New
Set in Adobe Garamond

Printed digitally in the United States of America

Library of Congress Cataloging-in-Publication Data

Journey, Anna, 1980–
If birds gather your hair for nesting : poems / by Anna Journey.
xii, 90 p. ; 22 cm. — (The national poetry series)
ISBN-13: 978-0-8203-3368-7 (pbk. : alk. paper)
ISBN-10: 0-8203-3368-9 (pbk. : alk. paper)
I. Title.
PS3610.O94I38 2009
811'.6—dc22                          2008048667

British Library Cataloging-in-Publication Data available

*for Greg Donovan*

# Contents

# Acknowledgments

Grateful acknowledgment is made to the following publications
in which some of these poems have previously appeared: *American
Literary Review*: "If Birds Gather Your Hair for Nesting"; *American
Poetry Review*: "The Nurse's Diagram of the Tracheotomy"; *Barn
Owl Review*: "Birdstorm," "Return as Black Currant"; *Best New Poets
2006*: "Lucifer's Panties at Lowe's Garden Center" (reprint); *Best New
Poets 2008*: "Adorable Siren, Do You Love the Damned?" (reprint);
*Blackbird*: "Clockwork Erotica: Why He Takes Off His Glasses When
Telekinesis Fails," "Elegy: I Pass by the Erotic Bakery," "He has given
his face to the waters of the lake," "Letter to the City Bayou by Its
Sign: *Beware Alligators*," "The Mirror's Lake Is Forever," "Night with
Eros in the Story of Leather (2)"; *Diner*: "Carnival Afterlife," "Corpse
Flowers and Grackles"; *FIELD*: "A Crawdad'll Hold Until It Hears
Thunder," "My Great-Grandparents Return to the World as Closed
Magnolia Buds," "Rose Is Dead and Crashes the Party"; *42 Opus*:
"Dissecting the Automaton," "Nude Girls to Pluto," "Red-Haired
Girl Wants You to Know"; *Gulf Coast*: "Autobiography as Endless
Calico," "Lucifer's Panties at Lowe's Garden Center"; *Hayden's Ferry
Review*: "A Skulk Is a Group of Foxes"; *Indiana Review*: "The Foot
Wing of Carolina's Artificial Limb Factory"; *Kenyon Review*: "Adorable
Siren, Do You Love the Damned?"; *Makeout Creek*: "Fox-Girl before
Birth," "The Shapeshifter Introduces Her Village to the Moon"; *Mid-
American Review*: "Birdskull, Cedar, Rosemary, Stone" as "*Ars Poetica*,"
"Elegy: After Filling Out Egg-Donation Forms"; *Poetry Southeast*: "A
Rabbit Must Be Walking"; *Shenandoah*: "Walking Upright in a Field
of Devils"; *storySouth*: "Backwater Blues"; *Sycamore Review*: "Sappho
on the Edge of the Bayou"; *Waccamaw*: "Drowned Angel Blues," "The
Gypsy's Late Arrival."

"Sappho on the Edge of the Bayou" received the 2005 *Sycamore Review*
Wabash Prize for Poetry, judged by Tony Hoagland.

"Carnival Afterlife" and "Corpse Flowers and Grackles" received the first place award in the 2007 *Diner* Poetry Contest, judged by Betsy Sholl.

With deep gratitude and affection for my teachers Gregory Donovan and David Wojahn, and to Virginia Commonwealth University's creative writing program. Warmest appreciation for Beckian Fritz Goldberg, the Corporation of Yaddo, and all the folks at *Blackbird* for their friendship and support, especially Mary Flinn and Susan Williams. Thanks to Mark Doty, Tony Hoagland, and the University of Houston's creative writing program. My thanks also to Thomas Lux. I'm grateful to the numerous writers who've helped me in workshop. Love to my parents; my sister, Rebecca Journey; Patrick Turner; Alicia Erickson; and Michele Poulos.

ONE

# Adorable Siren, Do You Love the Damned?

—BAUDELAIRE

The devil pries open my red hibiscus like skirts. On the crack
    corner those transvestite hookers won't quit
competing with my garden's

barbed and carnal tongues. The bitch
    scent of the silver-

and-pink-clawed possum in heat—all rhubarb-breath and unbelievable
    udder—is sharp as fuchsia

spokes of my oleander. I could put
    my eye out looking. I could run with knives. Outside the brine

of b.o. tangles with perfume—bodies that snag
    men like my singing

can't. This song won't dress up, won't wear black
    patent leather, won't even shave

its five o'clock shadow—lazy sliver
    slumming the telltale animal. What song, devil, is best
sung from my balcony

in my birthday suit, by my heartleaf nightshade's
    liquory patina? I'm drunk,
though I won't wear heels, honey, or I'd fall

for anyone. I'd fall devil
   over heels over edge over oleander
over open mouth

over birthmark over forked
   tongue over forked tongue
that turns on mine.

# Lucifer's Panties at Lowe's Garden Center

I told the serial killer he could feed his Venus flytrap Spam
    the summer I worked the outdoor lawn

and garden center. I'd known to say this since fifteen, with my mother
    telling me
        all men who ask young girls directions
from their white vans are murderers. Especially ones

wearing an arm in a sling who ask you to carry things. This one asked
    about hibiscus.
        I said *Rum Runner, the Fifth Dimension, Eye of the Storm.*

The flower with my own name, *Anna Elizabeth*, was too damn pink
    and ruffled. I switched
        its label, wrote *Lucifer's Panties*, stuck its white plastic
flag back. I named others *Unquenchable Burning, Hellflames,*

*Fire on the Back of Your Dark Tongue.* He wanted instead to apologize
    with the crepe-yellow hybrid for a woman

whose dining room window he'd shattered with a corner of drywall.
    He asked
        if the gift was a good idea. I told him he was going to need
a good pot—one with an angel,

copper frog, fat gnome, or fairy: *Girls love that shit.* Probably terracotta.

His slung arm—likely struck by lightning from handling Bluebeard's
    hoard
        on the aluminum bed of his construction van.
I helped him repot. The killer grasping the flowers' pale trumpets, me

tamping the dark roots. Before he left, a turnip moth

played the wind chimes above the register without touching them.
I pointed to the label, *direct sun*, but couldn't say,

Bring the blooms indoors before the frost.

# A Rabbit Must Be Walking

To swallow a chicken heart whole in its glue-skinned
pericardium is to believe the pickled chill

on the way down is love. That's why I shuddered
for no reason and knew

a rabbit must be walking on my grave—its sick
cotton a white flag, a peony. Who would believe it?

The black-eyed peas I ate in the New Year brought rain,
brought a basket of dried figs back to life

as they bloated over the picnic table's cedar boards.
I believed myself at thirteen

cursed by my red hair, cursed as my aunt's
one derelict rose—varicose coral

while the rest of the bush grew white as my scalp
under lemon juice, peroxide. My hair bleaching

in its own votive light. When the moon
is slung so low it becomes a song,

shrinks the blue spruce sapling into a white dwarf,
I know the magic half of my cracked penny

sewn into the boy's left sleeve must still be there.
But the shirt must be

in a thrift store by now, to be worn by hundreds
of men who pass me on the street and must pause

under the copper weight of it. They must all love me
like something hidden, even from their view.

# My Great-Grandparents Return to the World as Closed Magnolia Buds

They're not quite buried
in this cemetery, though they follow the afternoon
noise of bulldozers like tip after tip

of white-tailed deer disappearing.
They're back
by the soybeans, edging the delta from the dead,

keeping their clammy petals pulled
shut, like Klan hoods. A language
they labored to forget—Swedish was Natchez silt,

loam in the throat
their children never spoke.

I know the spicebush swallowtails flutter like angels
over the wood ducks' pond,

that the scum's slow ripple
is the alligator case of my grandfather's harmonica
and its chromatic shift

back and forth to sharp.

Though magnolia buds are too awkward
and pungent for angels, I know

they could hold the blood of a woman
or a man
like the gauze pads

she used in Germany to patch shrapneled
eyes of soldiers before knowing
the right place. Because this is the right place,

the wrong time,
the lapse of decades a salt brine between us—
four generations

of women linking arms. In the photograph—with me,
unborn, the bark hardening on a sycamore, dry wind
over the bayou,

the palsied cotton just about to fall.

# Fox-Girl before Birth

When the fox-girl lost her fur
in the third trimester
she was already too human
to stay in the life
before birth that is all
swarm and sea
dark enough to breathe,
before she lost her body
that was everycreature—the wide
Chinese fans of her gills, rose hipped
with spidery inks, her prehensile
tail's little finger joint
crooked for swearing, her blind
vole-eyes like steamed
black-eyed peas. Then she was
whole and good enough
to eat—those webbed palms,
her frog dive deep into the well,
the golden ball of her face
at the bottom.

# Drowned Angel Blues

My wings are invisible—
like the infinite, juiced-up
gloves of hummingbirds, or plums
bobbing in stirrups
of milky current. As a child, I once
observed a wasp hover
near a bulge in a picket fence—
some weird cocoon a housepainter
froze to the wood with his hurried
lead-based strokes. The wasp's
falter over the mummy
in the fence was like the boy who held me
at the dance, at thirteen, whose eyes
buzzed some distant target—another girl's
window of perfume
fracturing the dark room's blue
crepe-strung corners. One
partner is always better
at vanishing. I imagined, afterward,
that my wings could break
through my lead-white dress—could even
make headlines: the teen
in her borrowed antique gown
who entered the too-high river. Unlike the spun
moon in water—my fringe of eyelets
dragged like frozen rabbits. I knew
my wet lace at nightfall must hold
the most radical weight.

# Autobiography as Endless Calico

It never bothered me the little Dutch girls had no faces—
my quilt—a pink appliquéd length of them

bonneted blind. Or the fact they had no fingers
or elbows—hands folded to snowballs

on their still bells of skirt. Each one a mockery
in miniature, made of my mother's childhood

dresses. My favorite among them, mild as wheat, a scrap
of aged yellow, my calicoed rose.

No radical sweetness, no radish-mauve
billow of baby skin—it was the natural perfection

of sunned cotton, calla lily sprung late in the shade—
the last patterned girl I saw each night before sleep.

With dawn the old woman on my chest withdrew
to the blood-cherry rise of my teak cabinet's stain.

Nightmare trails—she was never really there. At eighteen
I worked the damp calico of the garden section

at a hardware shop, cement floors the color
of night terror. That work was a kind of sleep disturbed

only by the cash register's chimes. A man looking for the exotic
clematis asked me through daydream if I knew

the Pre-Raphaelites. He said I looked as if I'd stepped out
of an oil to stand beside the plastic display fountains. I said, *Yes,*

with the hiss of water in my red ears, *my cherubim
ran off with my bonnet and left me with nothing*

*but the whiteness of my sun-blocked sulk, my red hair,
my beguiling eyes.* No, I didn't say that. I squinted

for sun, deadheaded stalked shells of geraniums,
offered my childhood another dried bouquet.

# Letter to the City Bayou by Its Sign: *Beware Alligators*

Pimp's-hat shadows in the feathery date palm. Everything,
I think, at this illegal

hour in the public park has
a half-drunk gait. Dear slow, dark water, why hesitate

like an older man's hand on my thigh? I'm not sixteen and I'm
gin-brave since hopping the cyclone fence. Are you near

starved for my face in the water? Dear clear, single rose
that blooms in toxic bubbles

from your surface. Dear black bayou, once, by a river
I bit a man's neck. His scent: the raw

teak air husked inside stomachs of six
Russian nesting dolls—the ones in the attic I pulled

apart and open. The ones I
pulled apart and open like Styrofoam cups

stacked in your red-clay banks. Though I'm not
Russian, I can last all night

in an icy wind in nothing
but beggar's rags or my blue bikini. I'm made

of so many girls I can't get them all
drunk at once or they'd mutiny. Dear underworld, I'll sit here

all night with my selves jumping out
like gin from my tipped cup. You'll catch us one

by one. We'll lie in your hot shallows and, with our
dark smiles, raise your pulse.

# Visitation of the Rose

She left the body as wet jasmine
dazzles the green door
of the antique shop. She left the body
as she left the city: making lists,
last sights. The shop she'd never
entered before—its shelves of silk
fans, turquoise corsage
hazeled into fennel, lint blossomed
as the lapdog's one good eye. Vain
little shih tzu sniffs the rose
patterns of the love seat with no
ghost radar. Ouija with its vowels
scratched off. She spells *brrr* and *shhh*,
and so the dog must imagine the jasmine's
torn hem slides—deliberately—its cold
weather under the door.

# A Skulk Is a Group of Foxes

but one is *fabulous*,

we say, meaning *mystical*
or *fablelike*. In the backyard the stone pine blues
from the red fox that flares behind it.

Scientifically speaking,

we say *vulpes vulpes* sounds sexual,
or *Star Wars*, too much
animal at once.

You know repetition

without variation
is death. You know repetition
can be conversation: three to five syllables
stretched over Fox Canyon. Their sound—
wow-wow-wow.

The alarm bark—

monosyllabic. For danger. At close range
the sound is the cough of a dogwood stick
scraped across a picket fence by a girl.
She runs home from a white van she believes
is filled with murderers. They shout,
How to get to the interstate? after her, half
in Spanish, wave a blue and yellow map.

Translation.

The American poet asked the translator what her fox
sounded like in the version of her poem
in German. The answer: it barked
because foxes can't shriek in Europe.

Gekkering:

stuttering, throaty noise
from aggression, or it's courting season, or it's the boy
Kafka stammering
when his father enters the room.

Apparitions:

the red-haired grandfather I've never seen
with actual red hair
because it was always white, but knew
the story. And my grandmother's mink
that crept from the closet at night.

A picture'll last longer

than the fox's shy dance with the neighbor's
half-chow chained
to the winter crab apple that's erupted
into a yellow cloud. My
yelp at noticing them
unlit the flame under the pine, then the slow
sliding door's glass thunder.

The next time

someone says, *Don't skulk*
*in the doorway—come on in*, you'll know
they've conjured the animal.

# Apparition with Toenail Music

The drummer's strung goat
toenails click; the instrument
tapers like grapevine. In the jazz club
this is the sound: village

in the storm
of Jupiter's red god-eye, sound as hoofed

devil disappearing,
reappearing. I pretend
I don't know the reality
of sheep-gut, cat-gut strings, or gazelles

stretched over drumheads. Horsehair wiring out
the violin's voice. My psychiatrist

grandfather used his cadaver's
bones from college as an ashtray—
skull tipped on the coffee table. This is also

the sound of devotion. Stravinsky wanted the E-flat

clarinet solo in *Rite of Spring* to sound
like asparagus shoots growing. I've learned the last

four bass notes in English
spell *dead*, but isn't the catch
Stravinsky spoke Russian? Here, the music

shakes its claws, click of old calcium
that keeps growing after,

and after, the old wives say. This is how I watch
my grandfather

tap his yellow toes
on a footstool embroidered with large
mauve roses. From the black

balcony those toenails take on
any color of light.

# Corpse Flowers and Grackles

Their cries want to be something else—the shrill of brakes, a crooked
cop's static, the thump of a convict's body off Highway 1
down outcroppings of pink granite. Years ago you heard them

in Greenwood, Mississippi.
The sky's wrinkled cornflower—the blue

of your aunt's prison nurse pantsuit. Her stubborn refusal to name
anything: her two mean mutts called *Hey Dog!*, her half-Persian cat,
*Little Girl*. Even the stringy pot plants sagged

like battered palms between oaks, ignored.
What couldn't be ignored: The story of her son

shooting a man outside a bar in Jackson, the scent
of the corpse flower—its tropic rot. Her library filled with world
    records,
medical oddities. Your sister and you decide the biggest
flower in the world is enough

to hold buckets of dead birds, a body stashed in Sumatra, or a cousin
who'd crawl inside the flower to escape. The smell
must be ground-fall festering. Who ever thought the afterlife

could smell like this? In the garden of paradise
the grackles dancing look like dead birds—
necks snapped back—they offer this ritual everywhere,

unhindered by traffic, black ballets in the spear grass.
Decide: grackles are better at being grackles
than being resurrections of your grandparents, for who would have
   ghosts utterly

uninterested in the living, ones that make such noise? Now, you are
   uncertain
about the scent of the corpse flower, whether it reeks

from standing water, a dark bird dunked in its fetid basket,
or its own body, its own body that, when it opens,
lets everything in.

TWO

# The Shapeshifter Introduces Her Village to the Moon

Of course the spirit of the fox
sang as he entered the ink-haired girl

by prying up her fingernail's
cellar door, pale as a one-chicken moon
over her cooper father's workshop in Nagasaki. Let's believe

his woodblock prints of a red fox snowing white
plum blossoms in the dark forest meant the end of winter.
In the other prints, his red-headed Dutchmen are rendered
from life—the others imagined

from gossip: grotesquely white, red-haired barbarians.
Did you hear

when the cooper found his daughter—who could not read—
sprawled nude in his bentwood
cedar bathtub she had solved

his rosewood puzzle box by matching up
the written and carved names of berries

to cure ringworm? She said the cedar's sharp
smell caused her to claw the tub's sides until her fingertips
grew dark as hard southern cherries and her jaw

snapped from its back molars, volewide,
those front milk teeth tapered

like Western candles. Her dark hair was shocked into the ginger
of naked camphor wood so that her father's painter friends
took her for the Dutch consulate's mistress,
who, when vomiting sake into the still, green water, flipped

an entire ornamental pond
of ancient goldfish belly up. Her drunken dance after the cooper
kicked her from his house for madness

revealed the nine tails supernatural foxes gain
after living a thousand years
hanging from her skirts—also, a pearl-inlaid telescope
she introduced to the village

to bring the moon to rest
in her father's red bathtub at midnight.

# The Mirror's Lake Is Forever

That's when I knew the mirror was all sex and hard
fact. Unlike knowing my grandfather

posthumously. Because a ghost can't be
androgynous as a lamp is,

as peat moss is,
as the smell of cedar—

knife-feathery. Because the dead
can watch me pee without

even a trace of embarrassment. And who
has the right to more? Mirror

that couldn't reach my dead
grandfather's closet—his jewel-colored

medical books in former editions,
his gay porn magazines: men smooth

as conchs in soft-core seascapes. My mother,
who found them while cleaning

out his house, asks, *Are you sorry
I told you?* I said, *No,*

*I'm not sorry.* As if staring
into his horn-rims and my grandmother's

coral dress could help me understand
the selfishness of portraits—

their shut door splintering the past's
exact coffin-space.

I know that shame
is beard-high with two daughters—the blonde

one with cats and the dark one with red-
haired girls. I know

the mirror's lake is forever
dragged for corpses, lily-buoyant

arteries, livers, and cocks. I know
he's caught there: doctor,

with his white coat and gold-veined
tobacco. And what is more haunted

than the smoked voices
of cicadas under plums? And what

heats faster than silver? His constellation:
cold instruments raised

over useless space. Somewhere
there's a ghost

I'll open my shirt for, recount my
Entire Medical History for,

who I'll forgive for wearing
tweed and love beads and for hiding

stacks of magazines in the dark, who will press
that silver scope to his ear, who will listen.

# He has given his face to the waters of the lake

and his pear trees to the bedsheets
before frost. The whole dwarf orchard draped
in cotton. My grandfather has given shape
to the ghosts by the lake, unclaimed by kudzu, one
jutting fruit organ for each inch—each pear-fisted
heart and a heart, nipple stemmed. It's too racy
to watch, even in memory. My mother
has given her knuckles to the boy on the school bus—
the groper whose hand was a salamander
on her thigh's shy hem. The boy who gave
his jaw to the shocked look of violet
the river dazzles. My aunt has given her fugitive
son his escape to a Mexican schoolhouse,
his acned face to the choleric
yellow brick. He teaches English—
he has given the language
to the metal whirring of bikes
and a backwater. He has given his girl's lover
a blown-off leg beside the bar, pink
kneecap to the magnolia's flower. On my walk
through the graveyard, I have given
his slang to the dead Confederates: *Y'all,*
*come back now, come back*, who never listen—
my whispers to the silence
of the pear tents' inner weather.

# Charm against the Dead's Interference with the Satellite

The chicken wire cross her father pitched
on their cinderblock fence faces the Confederate graveyard.

While he nails drywall for the den extension, she reads

Donne's poem about a man who had a wreath
of his mistress's hair buried with him. The white, ironwork

porch chairs fill with beech leaves, and her father
dances a ladder to tilt the satellite dish.

&

He believes in music. He's strung
pierced beer cans with fishing line
from the gutter, golden with windfall pecans.

His daughter quit her job this morning giving tours
of the cemetery, watches their albino pit bull pace
the chain-link's knotty vineyard with a hard-on.

&

The red-eyed dog hears the 5:20 coal train from Petersburg
and barks before the girl looks up from her book,
the animal's white jawline ruddy as the sun's
raw strip over the river.

&

She smiles, remembers what she told
the old ladies bused in from Goochland about the dead
buried there, how *graveyard* is such a distasteful word.
The *memorial garden* is landscaped
in the *rural style*.

*❧*

*You'll find most of the dead women*

*named "sea of bitterness" or "my God is an oath." How's that*
*for your holy mother? I've read*

*from a most reliable source*
*that a man once took a wreath of his lady's hair to the grave.*

*When they opened it during the flood to rebury him,*
*his beard had grown to his pockets. The surprise is*

*his hair was blond until it touched hers,*
*when it flared into the mirror of newly minted copper.*

*❧*

The mausoleums gape on the hill, dark as sweetgum, and she's found
the second headless robin this week who remained
too late in the season. She's goddamn sick

of the purple bicycle with plastic lilacs in its basket
perched in front of the abandoned Victory
Rug Cleaners like a coy Victorian.

*❧*

Her father considers her a charm of sorts, something
the dead won't whistle through like a pork bone,

hex, or chicken wire, the chalky obelisks a collective
giving him the finger, his red-headed daughter who'd saw off
the top of the Blue Ridge with her stare.

*ᕲᕲ*

*Because they're like amaryllis*
*bulbs, the dead are only interesting midsummer,*

*when it's warm enough to tell stories about them. I used to take*
*the tourists to a certain grave by the river, tell them,*

*"Put your hands on the marble," just when I heard my pit bull's*
*bark. I'd tell them to wait for the ghost*

*to shake his raised grave, and each night*
*they could feel*

*in their palms his turn*
*as the train broke free of the dark.*

## Since the Rabbit Was Singing

I didn't hear my mother fly through the attic floor,
where she snapped

her vertebrae. My cartoons blared in the cool basement—
outside, the juniper's

inviolate hedge, its stinking blue border.
What gives, house? Why holes—the ceiling's

dark corsages—that suck
women in? What does this house think it's doing,
still bodiced

in water damage and poor boards? Those pink clouds
of insulation I stole

from the walls made one mean
Barbie heaven, those starry carcinogens

all phoenix, incineration. I chose my childhood
bedroom because the windows

opened onto bird's nest.
But look—the rabbit was singing

and dancing—it was tugging
on its flowered dress. And Mother, the house
refused to help you

float like that rabbit who, before he plunged
from the cliff's sheer drop,

cradled three
absurd seconds in pure air like the ticking
fish-eye of his ukulele.

Mother, this time
I swear I'll look up.

# Elegy: After Filling Out Egg-Donation Forms

### I. Colors: Family Medical History

Peach. Everything peach
or beige—the velour posture of my grandfather's armchair.

Or orange—their couch with its thin rust stripes. Even
the tugged velvet of her neck.

Ehlers-Danlos. The names of two men
who discovered my grandmother's skin disease. Her hands

were *extra* soft, my mom said. Loose joints, elastic skin. Almost
too soft to hold.

### II. Some of What I Write Are Lies

Why are you considering becoming a donor?
                                *I feel that I am exceptional.*
Do you drink to get drunk?
                                *No.*
Have you ever used marijuana? Even once?
                                *No.*
Are you a writer? What do you write with?
                                *Rainwater and a turkey feather.*

## III.  Cause of Death

An abdomen slowly filling with blood
feels like a full bladder.
After surgery, a nicked artery leaks
into the night. When
my grandfather rises, he makes it
to the hospital bathroom
before he realizes he's going to faint.
The emergency lever emits
a clear blue light. I wasn't there,
though I imagine the smell of green tiles
where he lay is Mississippi
suburban pines.


## IV.  Confessional 1

Barbie heads switch perfectly, though not
Barbie's and Ken's. What a freak show.


## V.  Confessional 2

Does it matter if a girl going 35 mph down the hill
on Roberts Road on a pink and purple bike

aimed for the telephone pole? And if she only
grazed a pink star on her elbow without

hitting the foot brakes once? Either way
she missed the target.

## VI.  What I Had to Look Up

My name
appears briefly in the New Testament
belonging to a prophetess who recognized
Jesus as the Messiah. Meaning: "grace" or "favor,"
but I'm a terrible waitress.

Rebecca—my sister, a "snare";

my mother, Cynthia, a "woman
from Kynthos"—mountain on Delos
where the moon goddess was born.

Dorothy, grandmother, a "gift from God." Does it matter
that I couldn't find my grandfather's name?

Does it matter that my father's name, Tim, is a nickname?
That it means "honoring God"?

I'm sick of all the godliness. Why can't our names
be the same as flowers or insects? Something
I might touch?

## VII.  Fall

I sang in the church choir with my hair dyed
neon pink. You heard me. The hole in the attic,

the hole in the attic, the hole in the attic
is a heaven
that spits you out on your back.

VIII. Prayer

For seventeen years I didn't know

the name of the ugliest flower in the world—mimosa trees
grew hairy by the sewer near my high school.

I'm writing a winter poem now—snow and stars,
stars as fractured vertebrae, the snow

as body cast, white back brace, machine—no,
I'm filling out forms—my family dissolving
with the earth, round as a wafer on their tongues.

# The Child Keats

The boy heard the calcium crack
of his father's skull on cobblestone.
Though he was at school in Enfield,
in a dream he knew wood doves
landing in the brittle arms
of a barkless aspen shocked an icicle
loose to stab into the soft rump
of a startled horse. The nudge of its
long face flashing in his father's
last landscape was his mother's
palomino throat—her secrecy
of birthmarks under crinoline.
This was the wrong season
for perfection, lovers, cowslips
in a field. He allowed the birds
their darting eyes, desultory
song—watched the white steam
rise from the horse's back.

# Birdstorm

Palm of no mercy. Palm the jaundiced color of wheat.
All day the lithium-edged cosmos hangs white

cloves of garlic in the lone birch's
albino limbs. I know that tree
knows lightning, just as I know the field cows hide

fingers in secret. Belly-palm,
palm of raw pink udders. Trigger-fingered snapdragons
torch the field at splendid

yellow intervals. Palm of catching
the crows as they fall. Palm of missing the bodies. Crows,

or the gesture of crows, furrow in turbulent, dark brows,
unfurrow in crowstorm

toward the rain cloud. All day the day after
my revolver leaves its scent streaking the wheat field,
the wheat stalks nearby

are tasseled in black powder: coal flowers.
I smoke in bed, as Gachet dresses

my chest, the nodule
the bullet nosed under my breast like a sharp blue koi
testing the pond's surface. Smoke rings

like agate rings for two days that lay amethyst
in layers around me. Halo the garlic knows as nightfall, the palm
   knows

as moving out into crows diving
toward the snapdragon about to fire.

# Snipers in the Arrangement

### I

Dumb cane: cause of the lost cat voice. The cry

will return as the poisonous plant
rinses free of your cat's larynx. For the larynx

lost briefly in toxins is not a real box, not something
to hide in, not something to wrap, not even the status
of scent. On the cherry table—the ferment of neon kumquats
in rum. Chewed leaf

of the dieffenbachia, meaning for hours
your first cat in childhood will have
no way to call you.

### II

An Easter lily's a simmering thing. The priest won't take them home

from the altar—released from their brass vase and green sponge
of artificial grass. Let thine tabby cat not vomit

stigmata for the lord's flowers. White blossoms
as kidney strickeners, as god

centered. Flowers
as snipers in the arrangement.

III

Dried jimson seeds hang redbirds without bodies
in the pin oak canopy. Your cousin, whose face swells

from allergy and hallucination, will shoot
someone's kneecap off

later at the dive. One more reason to move to Mexico.
Redbirds float like tomatoes

flung skyward by storm. The patch of creek-fed tomatoes
that knows what he'll do.


IV

Deadly cherry,
avocado, and almond. Deadly breadfruit,

elderberry, and lupine. The yew and the hemlock

and the weeping fig. The black cat crossing your path. To change your
    luck,
run backward.

# The Gypsy's Late Arrival

With her swallowtail skimming the goat milk,
that first surface of blue, she offers

to read my future in her slate-bottomed pail. *You're late,*
I say in the dream,

*my mother's back*
*has already healed.* Her white brace, bust shaped,

stands in the closet among the wooly peacoats. It crawls
like a white tortoise toward

the gypsy's violin-calloused hands. She coos
oil shale and limestone, steam

from the Estonian bog like unraveling sheep. I tell her I won't go
to the Italian place

with the full copper bar because it smells
like blood since the surgery. *No,* she says. The smell

is wild mint in a white-peach orchard, the aged
coal trains dragging their strata

of almond-colored smoke. The dusk plums
darken the field like a medical student's

cut-paper organs,
all labeled in hard Latin. *If I had a little girl,*

the gypsy says, tracing my spine, *I'd name her*
*Vertebrae: vertere, to turn.*

# THREE

# A Crawdad'll Hold Until It Hears Thunder

Don't speak
     rudely to the dead, you whisper,
as if humor goes with the soul. Say soul is a crawdad scared
     backward into the sawed half of a beer can,

caught by drunk teenagers across the river. Say I'm a reckless carp for it,
     color blind to its particular spectrum of red:
blood orange, bike rust, the cemetery

rose. You know walking past the graveyard plot named Slaughter
     is a kind of peasant's armor. Who could afford
such crypts?

     And God bless the poetry on such epitaphs:
a giving person, a kitten in each arm. In medieval times poor archers

stitched lengths of crawdad carapace into breastplates
     that were effective at stopping arrows
shot past fifteen yards. What did they do, then,

when death knows each scurrying
     crustacean as a mask? Conqueror, ten-foot
money-shot. I'm an amazing,

fish-boned motherfucker for it. We'll walk past,
     laughing. We'll return.

# Return as Black Currant

Because she bleeds dark jelly and French liqueur,
because she won't rise

to the stand of red alders,
she waits
for the devil's breath, that ocean-shunt air
from the coast,

to salt her body
ragged in its new forest, its high shade
space under persimmon. Before,

on her deathbed, she swore to return,
remembering

how black currant flowers grow in strange

bouquets, their berries
holding the smallest bones,

how it would take
only a ghost breath to move them.

It's impossible
to keep her from sliding out

seeds into that first layer of snow—
white on white—
femurs for strength

through winter. A little wine puckers
her mouth, her smile's
blood corners. There's no

westerly wind just yet, and the deep green
currant leaves begin
to sing on their small saws.

## Sappho on the Edge of the Bayou

Coughed up the jazz band's brass throats,
weddings are a hollow music
pressed thickly around curls
of the wrought-iron gate,
the cast-solid magnolia. There is rust
coppering down the fine
edges of everything here
in this violet light—the white pickup's
eaten paint, rose ash of cinder blocks,
the one cool sting
of dill on my palm. I wave
good-bye to you as the stone
face of the swamp refuses
your far-off reflection. It's better
this way. As you leave under
that snow of thrown rice, your veil
is the thinnest fishing net. Gongyla, arm
in arm with a man whose vow
grows heavier midair—it hangs
there like a darkening
smile, sweat on the edges
of your gown. This is the song I write
for your wedding, love, as pyramids
rise and weather: when willows
strangle the water pipes, a kiss
of cornmeal on your brow.
Now I wipe a stone bird's wings; now
the washboards miss a beat. With this
song I am snapped
loose like the sheep-gut
strings of a lyre.

## Rose Is Dead and Crashes the Party

My miscarried sister wants to be an owl—

At the costume ball, she's pressed against my basement's
white wall, raises the fluttering

mask of an io moth
to the would-be

of her cheeks, her not-yet
nose's Swedish hook

sharp on the scent of the before
and afterlife.

Some people
have all the luck. The glut of her look's

pure-helium-and-paper bird,

startling some brief
mardi gras

each time the sun strikes. This is the part of the ball

where no one
asks me to dance and I sip my wine

like it's asking for it, like lips
are the right answer. By now, I'm mean

and drunk and say,
*Some owl, sis. Christ.*
I say, *Get a life.* When she flies off,

the whole room
watches her eyes, heavy lidded and green as sweethearts—

I'm damn jealous. Her face, painted in god's
near-perfect drag,
comes close to the real

thing, but still the tongue-
tied animal.

# Elegy: I Pass by the Erotic Bakery

The way the tits of lemon meringue whorled

in the window that day
looked at first like breasts, then more like paws of my grandfather's

clubfoot Siamese.
I want to believe that, after he died, the cat didn't

gnaw off his face. I've heard it happens. I'd like to ask the pastry chef

if his vision of whipped
egg whites and sugar meant he saw, in a dream, that mangled paw

pressed to my grandfather's chest.
I know my grandfather

died alone, with the tv on. I need to know
he kept his face that day, in the green armchair, that the channel
he chose as his heart slowed was not

televangelism, but a bird documentary: dark-eyed juncos
jilting the magnolias, fiercer than angels

flying south. I need to know the show's voiceover
was pitched in the gauzy

timbre of lullaby—low and Latinate, Byzantine. Because
hearing, during death, is the last

faculty to go. And so, his last moments
were filled with the wing beat of juncos, and a calm,

omniscient voice: *Fringilla nigra, ventre albo*—*black
finch, with a white belly.* Languid in heat, the meringue
breasts cave a little, almost inscrutably

burnt brown at the side seams, and at the tips. I lick
my lips, though I
won't enter. I'm afraid

like Christ they'd turn
to flesh in my mouth.

# The Nude Model, Scary Mary,
## Shifts on Her Satin Pillow

The old art school terror—
that rare, embarrassed
glimpse during life drawing class. I vine charcoal

*azure shadows* under her
butt cheeks rimed in fluorescent, each one's wily
edged desert state. I draw

*the old woman form that fell*
*into the stark*
*wattage of a stare.* Scary Mary

meets my eyes, her unnerving
gaze over paunch, over pubes. *And when the muse*

*opens her bourbon*
*rose thighs?* I don't ask the teacher. And he doesn't say,

*Draw her hair the color of dry*
*clove catching.* She's multiplied

and filled the room
with her cigarette mouth's loose pucker. He
shows how to measure

her proportions from a held-up finger, requires nudity
for homework. Let's
you and I lie

flat as the second
dimension, honey,
move like the third. Let's throw our clothes

in a pile
and draw them burning.

# Night with Eros in the Story of Leather (1)

You swagger in late, devil, trace with your tail
shadows: those sexual edges

a black tupelo throws under the balcony. You carry a copper bowl
of Italian lemons, and yellow thumbprints

of jasmine oil drag under each ear.
I demur, say the balcony

isn't orchard enough, isn't sultry enough, though the one-eyed
stray's pheromones could flame

from my heel's strike. Desire begins here
in bondage, in bougainvillea and its blunt mists

of ammonia that cuff my burning
eyes like a bride. Devil, I feel your svelte double crossings

rise from the coral bell vine. You lisp dusk
outside my door, drive lightning

through my cobalt window. Your harsh accents boil
honey from the dark

of my mason jar. Devil, hold me like bread
between your six gold teeth,

like the wet leaf
that sidles by with its butcher's serrations,

dares my tongue's red
leather to tie you.

# Clockwork Erotica: Why He Takes Off His Glasses When Telekinesis Fails

The white heather nods like automata
under my cypress. In my dream their calico
light in the antique theater is not enough
to dim the carved faces from two
wooden lovers—wound by clockwork
to perform sexual acts. The men
in the audience smell blackly
of cognac and bay leaves once
souped in my wet hair. I know a widower
sits beside me by the waft of nutmeg
tucked in his pocket—an apron's secret
lavender ties. From the second row he fails
to break the grand crystal chandelier
with his stare and removes
his glasses. The artificial woman's
moan hole, ovaled in planes of young olive,
blurs to his dead wife's parted lips,
their spittled edges. I know she once raised—
with her breath—a steaming
loaf of rough-grained pumpernickel,
that whole black hill, cooled.

# Gachet Dresses the Wound

Smoke rings the grey of orchid shadow
in weak light—in wheat field light
blowing through windows. The day
before dying, Vincent, I watch you smoke
all day in bed. Smoke rings that, widening,
dwarf your wounded body
like some wizened Saturn becoming
less and less of a planet, more
stardust. More the breath of yellow
fennel knocked through your window
by a tolling Auvers bell. Three fingers
of pitch—the space between
your lips like Adam's finger gap,
the god-gap. The wound's clearing
in your chest hair—a fire-cleared field.
The bruise spreads as if in linseed oil, layering
the bullet's blue almond. You wave—
not at me—and your fingers
sever one ghost-plumed ring.

# Night with Eros in the Story of Leather (2)

> *We do*
> *lose what we never had.*
> —BECKIAN FRITZ GOLDBERG

To exorcize my demon, he licks
the edge of my widow's peak

in the middle of a winter cotton field. His hot tongue
slurs ivory

goats of steam
from my forehead. They rise, sinuous
as scents of gin off the junipers—little

mouthfuls burning. He wants my
latest confession. I say, *Fine*
*but no kiss—*

only leather: muzzle, bit, collar to wrist,
wrist behind back, behind silver-

spiked bodice. *Do you mind if I enter*

*your dream?* he asks. The one where the holstein
is stung by barbed wire. She drags her blue
entrails smoking through the ginger grove. *Do you mind*

*if I interpret?* I gag him, grind my

red boot over breastbone. He dreams the smell of ginger root
cracked by the panicked

cow's hooves, her scattered
blood iron in the spear grass. Then, his breath
at the back of my neck, his glance

choke-chained, breathlessly

telepathic. My demon
stamps inside like a starved goat—black

hoof on my tongue,
its bitter eggplant. My lips
won't hold long

their cloven shapes
or his song: *Blue thistles*

*bloomed in cities.* I can't stop—
the story

going like the tongue goes:

lit and loosed, moving,
like Lucifer,
down.

# Walking Upright in a Field of Devils

Because billy goats rise to the height of a woman
and walk upright, I saw a field of devils,

blue and vertical, horned in the moonlight, heat
lightning in their luminous beards. Because the static

of grackles crying from ball moss in mesquite
meant this could be Italy, though it was the black

fields caught between strip malls
flanking Houston.

It's true that Keats walked further and further
from England into Scotland and the landscape grew

more grim with every step. Lakes shrunk to a slurp
in each cheek. It's also true

that ships from a distance bob as copper weathercocks
over the thatch of cottages. True, the prickly pear

is a leper dropping its limbs in the field. What is untrue?
The shape of a lung filled like a trough

might press down on a man's stomach—
he'd write his lover: a bellyache

brief as a devil's beard.
In the field: goat eyed and planetary,

something about to move, the half-bloomed moon,
a pecked-out tea rose. The sun still hours away

in another century—morning stalling its laudanum
eyes over a field, a deathbed. Bodiless.

Then the rise.

# FOUR

# Carnival Afterlife

*for Elmer McCurdy*

Because the corpse opens his mouth for change even now,
         decades after the embalmment, the fairy tale
lies there, nickel-thin

         filament on a mummy's tongue. I hear the best-dressed
bandit is a dead one

         strung in pinstripes in the corner of a funhouse. I like a man
who knows what he wants: a few jugs of whiskey, a night train
         robbed in Nowhere, Oklahoma.

Immortality like a wax stiff
         shot in the gut, a formaldehyde that lasts, and lasts longer
than a lover

         saying the sickle moon curls
back like a watermelon's scab-dry rind, and the dark

         glinting its slick night grease like a loosed
sideshow ermine. When the heart stops,
         it must be the sixteen-year-old girl has snuck

under the tent's side to stuff her fistful of late summer myrtle
         down the throat of the hanged man.

Those mouth-blooms were made for multiplying

in the hall of convex mirrors. The moment before
she was caught, the whole room
        reflected their fuchsia bouquet,

bigger than any plastic graveside flower,
        and he hung there, swaying from her touch.

## Madman and the Royal Shapes of His Cloud

A rain cloud drags its belly like a violet placebo
that withholds from me

its past lives—the diving
tortoise, deer hackles in shadow, the auroras dangled
by icy nectarines at noon. The convenience

store clerks guess the cloud's shape
is one hoppy breath from the madman's yellow lips. He leaves

the pawnshop's neon corner
each morning for forties and strawberry wine
the color of tubing from his chest,
once drained after surgery—some war. Only I guess

his past life as a drunk
nobleman who commissioned the most
accurate brass grooves to rise,

fleur-de-lised, from either side
of his bedchamber's keyhole. The bright paths in metal
steadied his hand, the aim of his key, no matter how dark

the hallway, how good the hunt, how much
banquet wine. Thunder unrolls

like sleeves, like an apricot
pulled from the starched ear of a peasant
by a man whose magical powers

made royal exits. But this is the wrong cloud, wrong century
keyholing pure storm—notchless—the locked
door back.

# Birdskull, Cedar, Rosemary, Stone

The punch line is it was in her handwriting,
though it begins

and ends with the early snow, star thistles
of breath against the sliding glass
door on the deck. This is long before

the war in Iraq, before my childhood
neighbor shaved his half-Japanese hair,

pissed his name into the fresh powder:
the name *Joseph* spelled
in shadows and air. He's waving

as he writes cursive, laughs with his back
toward me under the mulberry.

I'm a lapful of birdseed
closer to the scrap of suburban oaks
and laurel, to the male cardinal's delinquent

blood shot in the dogwood.
With the tin zip of his jeans he's closer

than ever now to saying it. What he wrote
was a worm
in the heart's wall

exposing the frozen ground—
its language of dark

and innumerable blades:
not I love you, not the Huck Finn raft we built
and sank last year in the near-dried creek,

but birdskull, cedar, rosemary, stone,
holding out a bare name.

# Nude Girls to Pluto

I shoved naked photographs of me
into the sewer
after the breakup to prevent

them from appearing
near ads for cello lessons
pinned in our grocery store. Though

it's true the prude
green bodice of winter corn could use
some daring rip, an exposed

nipple's pearl, and the juiced
pomegranates I'd name suitable
rivals for my lips, the puckered

money of the apple. My song went
*my clothes and books and drawings*
*he flung into the black street bellied up*

*white, like squirrel under hawk,*
*and the dirty photos he threatened to mail*
*to my father, la la . . .* We broke even

when I'd given my twenty-seven
secret positions
to the underworld, Kama Sutra

to the city's blue pipes—blue balls
to the ottoman's
jilted leather. I gave all my

nude girls to Pluto, the old
god-rock. My harem to the gutter rats'
black, forgetting river.

# The Foot Wing of Carolina's Artificial Limb Factory

*for Michele Poulos*

The white cellar's alien wattage
is myth bright over the rows of old ladies

hired to hand-paint details on the cast-
silicone feet. You tour

the assembly line, hoping
to meet the entertainingly grotesque. Instead,

the woman stoops
thinly over her magnifying lens, still

as a gilded tea-ware rim
lustered from the last century—

her time warp a polite line of china-painted
kittens on the kitchen sink and, by the bed, cat skins

netted in blue Asian paisley. You watch her white
hair weave through the dull teeth

of her tortoiseshell barrette, her violet pantsuit
zippered to collarbone. Can she tell if she holds a man

or a woman's limb tapering into fluorescence? She paints
only toenails, though, starts each time

left at the little toe and moves right. You move
close enough to see each nail bed's small

fan of pinks, and as she tilts the foot,
subtly, so as to avoid making it dance

a gruesome two-step across the starry
dazzle of Formica, she might chant,

*Sickle, sickle, sickle, gibbous, half,* to remember
each shape, each stroke of the three-haired sable

detail brush. She lingers
over the big toe's mock lunula as she names

the whitish moon eclipsing the cuticle, which is also the name
she gives the sugared drink she pours with bourbon

after her shift. And if she were a watercolorist
in Depression-era Burlington? You can hear lost trains

rattle mesquite pods along the dirt
road to her father's farmhouse, her father dead.

The trains cut the air clear as keratin
as a man's face peers out—the man

who'd become her lover for that one
drought-husked summer. You watch them Lindy Hop

under alders, stop, and she's fit her blue temple
in the hollow of his jaw—his scent:

hay bales and crushed mint dried
to the edge of a highball glass. And what if each toenail

she'd paint for decades after he left town was a white
sliver of his face on her peach gingham

slipcover in lamplight? Each toe, a miniature portrait—
him rising from the bed,

his cheek hard-angled and flushed from kerosene
in the blown glass, each painted artificial nail

ending on the same image: his vanishing
after the brass snuffer left its heavy

burnt-wick scent in the room. Or you guess
she paints instead the half-shadowed

dish of goat's milk thickening under the window—
the only moonlight you see glazing

the night's loose pitch across her body that will rise
alone with her bed stand's

blonde fumble of paintbrushes
stuck in the dark hole of a china cat's skull, the one

who stared him into a memory as she slept,
its fat face startled into orchids.

# The Nurse's Diagram of the Tracheotomy

*for Billy Strayhorn*

It was the way Sweet Pea sipped cognac
through his throat's clear tube—its thin amber

always catching the light under my adjustments—and the jazz
I recognized as his playing in the white room.

The diagram's black-and-white illustration drew
his eyes through horn-rims. The thyroid's blossom

hanging from the trachea's stalk
like a snowed-over crocus, stiff with ice,

its stem rimmed, the stoma a black hole
through his body's weather. That's when he began to mutter,

forgetting the void that had to be sealed
with a fingertip. His breath barely flapped

at his starched collar. All I ever heard was piano
stepping from some distant room like a dress. If I asked

him to repeat, he would point to the poster's stark human
silhouette, to its flower that grew inside,

meaning: *Lotus Blossom, Passion Flower, Flower
Is a Lovesome Thing.* A flower

will drink anything. My aging neighbor will put out
his last cigarette tonight

in the potted orchid's topsoil—the kitchen light
will shut off suddenly,

and I'll watch his picture window
a minute longer—the flower's pale outline turning

quietly to pitch. I'll wait for the dark that lightning
once sizzled into my den and what came after,

the grand's slow bank of ivory
glowing for a while after the lamp went out.

# Dissecting the Automaton

Thankless work. Like seeing only yellow
        scallops in the plant named *Cowardly Lion*. Later, I dream blue light

of a laboratory and a mechanical lion,
        stopped and splayed before surgery. I'm nurse, nurturer, old

knife-girl drawing the moon like iron through the far skylight.
   The vents sliding
       temperate breaths through metal.
I love an animal that'll open

       like a girl—that first cut into the lion's
mushroom-soft copper

with my oxblood razor. The rib cage opens like French doors
       onto a balcony strung with Christmas lights. The lion's eyes roll

their walleyed pupils of glass
       that even the opiates don't darken. What's found, what's given over

to the realm of the nurse's
       silver fingers tipped in mercury—a little manicured death
she sweats up in the dark. Sewn up, I sync

the lion's steps with the night garden's scents—its sterile
       black grasses, its curt
valves of lavender.

## Backwater Blues

The wisteria's dumb pendulum, lavender
too loud for thistles—all this,

and the moon isn't man or woman
enough to inspire song

from mockingbirds in August—silence
all molting season.

In my grandfather's Mississippi
orchard, there are two kinds

of apples: eaters and cookers,
two kinds of sisters
wading the kudzu path. There are turtles

the girls can tell
return each year because our red dots

stay inked on their shells. The smell of the Yazoo
will never leave—its black-eyed Susans
blunting the cherry picker, its rot

of wild dill. It's never enough
to remain

at the edge of the wood's
makeshift arbors—snapdragons
still as killers'

red vests in deer season. It's never enough to remain
in the body. A turtle's bare shell,

disembodied, backbone in high relief,
topsoil caught in the vertebrae—

while the mottled birds watch us
from the stand of live oaks—
we'll dig it out each time

like a dark song,
that whiskey on the tongue.

# Dark Mouth like a Lullaby's

The mouse enters the black mouth of the rosewood
      violin in its one body—exits

as a scattering of children, furred and slick
as my sleeping tongue. This happens with my grandfather's ghost
      when he enters

my throat, sometimes
      in the middle of dinner. When I say Venus

is unusually bright tonight in late spring and stare at the body,
illuminated—white rodent that floats

in my coffee tin brimming with chicken grease.
      Or there are many

toadstools, so we don't need umbrellas. Or a magnolia
      for each pitcher of milk in the humming fridge. In the hall
he is the veined

silver underside of mint leaves in the dark. My grandfather exits
      with the sound
      of an accordion's exhalations. Look,

when I shook his violin,
      the mouse children rolled from its dark mouth like a lullaby's
      good eye giving back

night its animals with one full look, the gut strings
nocturnal, plucked.

# If Birds Gather Your Hair for Nesting

Among other things,
you'll go crazy. How many thousands

of ancestors peer through you like a luthier
stooping for the right key,

the perfect hollow matched—
itself to itself. The dead must be beautiful,

you say. Hair is proof. Its fools' gold
catching in the car door. Dead, it keeps growing—

you know the tale. When you babysat three girls
and let them give all their Barbies mohawks,

they sobbed for hours when they saw
it wouldn't grow back. You can't curse

what you can't catch, so you've forgotten the sound
of the garage door opener,

the way your nose
is too long in photographs, the time a mockingbird

crapped right down the part of your long hair. You thank
no one in particular

for your inner French gypsy, Swedish nurse, the Confederate
cemetery one block away

that you love,
the brief warble on each side.

# Red-Haired Girl Wants You to Know

The sycamore mark on her inner thigh is a continent
about to divide itself into the angel
that sat in the votive light

of a fourteen-year-old's cigarette, and the angel
that was never there

but for the inked tattoo of wings under each blade
of a bartender's shoulder. Behind her eyes

there is a jealous god—
one wild swirl in each iris, each center a mix of pitch
and Byzantium about to catch.

There is a remedy for all of this
or none of it. An old man's advice:

don't let a morning pass
without swallowing nine
gin-soaked golden raisins. Do this to keep

arthritis at bay.
Or for the hell of it.

While she wonders why the only man to tell her

what's sexier than nudity
was an art critic and not a lover. She detests

the way red-haired women morph

into whores, sinners, or fox fur
shawls with the heads left on. Look, when that girl stared Zeus down
in all his glory, her hair was all flame for a moment.

And it was worth it.

Then dust. Then a poppy field with its charred seeds
between silks with a scent that could bring

the gods to their knees.